# WINTER COAT

Tom Whalen

Red Dust · New York · 1998

# ACKNOWLEDGEMENTS

Poems in this collection appeared in the following periodicals:

"So I Went Out Again" in *Telescope*, "Aubade (I)" in *New Orleans Review*, "On Robert Walser's Birthday" in *Maryland Poetry Review* and in *Crosscurrents*, "Getting Back to Him" in *The Southern Review*, "Exile" in *South Coast Poetry Journal*, "Winter Coat" in *The Burning World*, "The Master Says His Prayers at Night" in *Chelsea*, "Rehearsal for Another Extinction" in *Southern Plains Review*, "Kleine Wanderung" in *The Maple Leaf Rag*, "The Magician," "Tomato," and "Cosmology" in *Kestrel*.

*Winter Coat* by Tom Whalen
copyright ©1998 Tom Whalen

Published by Red Dust, Inc.
All rights reserved

ISBN 0-87376-086-7

# CONTENTS

So I Went Out Again . . . . . . . . . . . . . . . . . . . . . . .5
Aubade (I) . . . . . . . . . . . . . . . . . . . . . . . . . . . . . . .6
On Robert Walser's Birthday . . . . . . . . . . . . . . .7
Getting Back to Him . . . . . . . . . . . . . . . . . . . . . .8
Exile . . . . . . . . . . . . . . . . . . . . . . . . . . . . . . . . . . .10
Winter Coat . . . . . . . . . . . . . . . . . . . . . . . . . . . .11
The Suicides . . . . . . . . . . . . . . . . . . . . . . . . . . .12
The Master Says His Prayers at Night . . . . . . .13
Rehearsal for Another Extinction . . . . . . . . . . .14
Insects . . . . . . . . . . . . . . . . . . . . . . . . . . . . . . . . .20
Tomato . . . . . . . . . . . . . . . . . . . . . . . . . . . . . . . .21
Kleine Wanderung . . . . . . . . . . . . . . . . . . . . . .23
The Magician . . . . . . . . . . . . . . . . . . . . . . . . . . .26
The Topsy-Turvy Suicide . . . . . . . . . . . . . . . . .28
Cosmology . . . . . . . . . . . . . . . . . . . . . . . . . . . . .29
Aubade (II) . . . . . . . . . . . . . . . . . . . . . . . . . . . . .30

## SO I WENT OUT AGAIN

So I went out again in the liquid circumstances of
　　my life
and saw the happy orangoutang of my love
cleaning the sidewalk drains of their zeppelins
and winter shoved its shoulder against the door
and lo all around me the swimming trees
the scratch against the sky
then the quick shower of blood I thought was rain
the next pulse took me to the river
the next to your flooded heart
O child in the cupboard
you balance my days like plates
you stumble into the laundry of light

## AUBADE (I)

I remember nothing in the dawn,
the night only a flourish,
music without song,
a story I have unlearned.

A man in a taxi once lost,
or so he said, a sceptre
that made time do "whatever
I want it to, understand?"

I am not one to doubt,
but what was I to make of the cello
he held in his lap like a dictionary
or a loaf of bread or a child

whose sleep was so deep not even
the head-on collision awoke him.

# ON ROBERT WALSER'S BIRTHDAY

It is good, always, on April the fifteenth, to remember the apparitions who take time, in the corners of dust, to speak to me, often just before sleep, as if they wanted me not to remember them, or to think of them as the ghosts of ghosts. I do not think this plague of voices will be the death of me. I am comfortable in my robes, the wine glass has been emptied more than once, and these creatures knock about like clowns trying to sniff what remains in the glass. Of course "knock about" are the wrong words, their fingers pass through the chairs around my table like I imagine voices do when they are released from the mouths that have moored them—invisible birds flutter over my head.

Once I walked along the Rosenberg, the mountain upon which Walser died, and spent the night beside a ruin dated 878 A.D. Also I visited the asylum where he was housed the last twenty-three years of his life, and one of the attendants flattered me by mistaking me for a patient.

Sometimes I believe there is no sense left in the world.

I sleep in a back room, though I can't actually say what I do there is sleep. I drift, from night to night, year to year, listening to voices whose music is too pure for me to understand.

# GETTING BACK TO HIM

It takes longer than I remember,
like the train that went in circles
around a mountain I'd never seen,
and at the top was one of those old
medieval castles you see when travelling
up the Rhine. It's like a toy
you forgot in the rain and one day
you see it in some other kid's yard,
and you think it's yours, but
you're no longer sure. It could
belong to the kid with the missing finger
swinging in the low branches of a tallow tree.
And besides, you don't even know
if you want it, it's broken, its back
is cracked, its color gone. It's like
that, or something like that, trying
to get back to him, and you don't even know
why you try. He never held out his hand
with a ripe plum in it. He never wrapped
you up like a loaf of bread overnight.
When you clapped your hands or called,
he didn't come like a good dog. Instead,
he spun like a top. That was his game.
Spinning. You couldn't control him. You
couldn't walk away. He was with you
in his spinning, sucked you up

like you were flotsam in a whirlpool.
And now you want to get back to him.
What madness. What nonsense for the
birds to feast on, if there were any,
but there's only a little memory,
perhaps, something left over from dream
you can't quite dredge up, a glimmer,
tinfoil in the grass, light sluicing
all over the yard, and the boy spinning.

# EXILE

What if in the night you see that that's not the ceiling
over your head but a nest of pterodactyls

And what if your arm is not really an arm
but the still-warm muzzle of a shotgun

And if the moon out your window is not the moon
but the severed eye of your albino love

Then it is you who are not with us any longer
not your tongue or your language or your mind

You are lost a star without a universe
rotating out there knowing nothing

like a man drinking coffee at a desert café
dreaming of the map that'll take him home

# WINTER COAT

A. What is it made of?
Sounds left out back in the toolshed
where your father made you pray.

B. What is it made of?
The light under your door.

A. Who is its maker?
The ghost of your maternal grandfather
who told stories on the stairs.

B. Who is its maker?
The flies in the barn near the abbatoir
where you were born.

A. When was it woven?
The night your mother's lover photographed
her in the nude with your Polaroid.

B. When was it woven?
Before the flame touched your tongue.

A. How is it worn?
Over the shoulders of the wind.

B. How is it worn?
Like skin.

# THE SUICIDES

Who else leap to heaven but the suicides,
repeatingly.  Once there, the walls thicken,
and they must sing to get in, while inside
their predecessors pad about, as stricken
as they ever were, as they ever were.
Yes, much fun is still to be had, if only
the screen won't crinkle, the edges blur.
The hands tremble, extend beyond sight, simply.

Consider: I met one the other day.
Like me, he wore a coat, a hat, and had,
like me, a gift for little to say.
The rooms are nice, they fall apart.  Instead
of clouds there are clouds in the shape of clouds.
He continued: Everything is.  Nothing astounds.

# THE MASTER SAYS HIS PRAYERS AT NIGHT

It's a late supper I'm having before the night
takes off her clothes. This is the road to Heaven.
The stars freeze, the birds cock their heads
just so. I've taken this candle to the basin
where dawn lies scattered like ash from a pipe
my grandfather smoked before bed every evening
of his adult life, but always first he checked
this immense barometer he'd bought, a really big
 barometer it was, it showed him the ways
of the world in livid color, the way the snow
sometimes rises instead of falls, and the way
a staircase will lead as often as not
to nowhere in particular, the best spot
to make love. I confess I've murdered a couple
of wine bottles tonight, seized the trowel
and went to work on this song to delight
the eyes of She-Who-Is-Never-Here. I'll
spit a little into this glass, and paint
up a picture of vines and hexagons funneled
with the phosphorescent panic of young girls.
Then I'll load up this wagon with overgrown
loaves. What a forbidden ruin the world is!
In the dawn we always count on new blood.

# REHEARSAL FOR ANOTHER EXTINCTION
*(for the Brothers Quay)*

If I press here
        on this rubber tip
                of an old odd design
    where candle wicks,
          severed from bedsides,
                      tremble
in the one eye, the one
        tense
            tied to the heart
of a desiccated clock,
        then I am a wire candle
fluttering like a spider
        in the marionette's
                tight embrace.

A steam like grief rises here
            in this landscape
                  of pins against
this gray version
        of heaven
              and leaves.
A compass scurries
        across the plain,
               spiralling the sand,

mocking the wires.
                What is a pencil
                              without its puzzle
but a concentrate of attachments
                              minutely tiled
to reveal
        the slightest chip
                in the hourglass,
the stupefied
        lamination of fingers,
                      branching
from the shack of stuffed
                ostriches and
frayed rackets
        bent over
                some loud machinery of dread.

A ball
        bounces up steps
                to nowhere
                        or
to rooms of frozen furniture
                      painted egg-yolk yellow
to match the faces of a crowd
                      that's no longer here.
And then it hesitates,
        vibrates in the air,
                      with the air,

    a ball
            suspended
                        in air
beneath all these unstitched
                      distances,
                                      dismantled
attachments—
            but still,
                        a vibrating residue,
what remains
            in the particleless air.

Is it lightning
            that has emptied these pockets,
this glove
            in which a breath puffs up
                            a single finger?
The glove is vertical,
                  and somewhere
insects
            reverberate like ruins.

An oscillating fan
                  imagines its shadow
                              at every turn,
and with it
            we come back again,
                          but only to leave,

and then
> come back again—
>> repetition that allows itself
always
> only
>> the expectation of change.
>>> This turns
to waste,
> and this,
>> and this translates
>>> into an eye
attached to wires.

What effaces itself more
> than symmetry?
>> A fiber
in this space
> within spaces,
>> where at the end
of which space
> is a room,
>> remembers,
however faintly,
> the notation for S,
>> but imperceptibly,
like the movement of the fan—
> where does its turn end,
where does it begin?

    And if I enter this door?
                        There is no afterglow here.
  In one corner the remnants
                of a man
                        sleeps.
And against the back wall,
                another
                        rubs his forehead
between his eyes.
              In one corner
                      a man sleeps;
against the wall
          another rubs the center
                        of his head.
This is not memory.
              This is not
                    repetition.
I enter a room
        I've never entered before.
                        A man sleeps.
Another
      rubs his head.
              What is
                    the minimal
                            of I?
The man rubs his arm.
              He looks
                    left,

then right.
              The man
                       rubs his arm

and there is no depth
              to his breath,
                       no rain
to forgive me this mask
              plucked from whiteness
or a clay path
              singed with noon.
                       I will take
this one eye
              with me nowhere.
                       In my hands
I'll raise
       a sepulchre
              of horsehair
                       to the moon.

## INSECTS
*(for Linda Francis)*

There is a dent in this room, this air, and
I've come here anyway. You would understand,
but then so would a poor mirror were I rich
enough to own one. If a projectile as grand
as the Himalayas sailed over the roof of the world,
I'd take this as but a flutter, just another
dying inside. Insects, you said, come out
from my last breath. Well, yes. I can
see that. And all these non-insect heads filled
with courteous doubts corrode the molecules
we breathe as definitively as an atomic blast.
Let's set aside for the moment those clusters
of baby carriages, professions, and precautions,
and instead trace the shadows their wings make,
these hobgoblins without boots, marionettes
without hands, as concupiscent as spirals.

# TOMATO

Once, like all things, it was a single line, a tongue
down the spine, but now it makes a cloud, a surround
and a sound red as rain. It does in fact rain here,
from within and without, and within again.
A pulpy moon that fell to earth, was pulled
by the tides or, perhaps, a memory of tides,
which is what tides are. If it lacked wisdom
it would have been a stone, but wisdom we know
rains. And all this wetness is of the ocean.
No seed soaks so long; thus the fruit
could hardly be other than it is. Sweetly drunk,
like a monk, I encounter its perfection even
in my dreams. Not the rock-like apple, but this:
the embodiment of tautness. What else opens
the sky, lavishes the sun with such drippings?
It wants to fall, not orbit. If you wait long enough
with outstretched hand, it will come to you.
Such power in complacency! A mansion of suns,
or at least a rooming house where all the inhabitants
want to escape. A pressure outward, like the universe.
Perhaps, finally, a universe that will never collapse,
no matter whether drawn or quartered. It's skin
(the outer layer of the universe) a tension film
that, once broken into finite galaxies, star clusters,
will reseed the ether, reform space.

On this round table I've stacked several as high
as I can. When they fall, they do not bruise
like children or bananas. An adult object, then,
yet somehow (in song?) brother to the frog.
Birds search here for their liquid young.
Parenthood as perfection, but equally
something wishing to be held, handled,
laid in laps. Light gathers in its crevices.
Nowhere, not even when split open,
does darkness obtain. Light, as a liquid,
is not yellow; rain, as light,
is red—what surrounds the surround.
And, again, the sound a red song,
and a ripeness, which is what death is.

# KLEINE WANDERUNG

Odd how every time I sit down at this desk to begin
   my calculations,
my hand sinks through the lacquered wood into the
   fountain at Paradeplatz.
I pull it out, for it's excessively cold, this fountain, and
   let the pencil hover over the page.
But if I touch a number, the light shimmers off Lake
   Zurich
and a flock of *Taucherli* (little divers), or coots to us
   Americans—
their bodies black except for the white blaze of their
   faces and beaks—
run with their tiny feet (they are not fully webbed)
   atop the water.

A student knocks on my office door, but I have these
   grades to record by noon. Outside
I can't see the trees for the summery haze, although
   it's October here in New Orleans.
Ms. Altendorfer receives a B, but when I mark the letter in my ledger,
I step aboard the gleaming blue and white No. 9 tram
that takes me past the *Universität* and part way up the
   *Zürichberg*.
A young woman with a plaid cape smiles at me,
then lays her copy of the *Neue Zürcher Zeitung* on the
   seat beside her
(as if in offering, should I wish to take it)
and rises when the conductor sings out,
   "Winkelriedstrasse."
I can smell her freshly washed hair as she passes
and the hot chestnuts she holds in a little bag in her

hand.
I scoop up the paper, tuck it into my back pocket,
   and follow her out,
not to *follow* her, but because I know nearby
there's a bakery you like, the Vier Linden, and there
I buy two slices of *Birnenwähe,* a kind of fruit pie
whose filling *(Guss)* tastes like my mother's chess
   pies
(I've lost the recipe, and it's really unlike anyone
   else's).
And because the day is cool and I've on tennis
   shoes,
I decide to walk down to the old city, past the *Uni*
where students lounge on the balcony of the
   Mensa.
I see Katia there with her boyfriend in a distant cor-
   ner feeding the sparrows.
"Hello, Tom," she shouts, and I wave a greeting.
   She tells me
she saw you a few minutes ago heading down.
So I continue on my way, taking the steps one at a
   time,
and pass the *Bibliothek,* still under renovation,
and cover my ears to protect them from the pound-
   ing of a pile driver.
The *Wähe* is still warm in my hand, though the air
   off the river is cold.
For a moment (I don't know why) I doubt
whether you will be waiting for me at the fountain,
but only for a moment. You know I will be there,
and you left off work five minutes ago in order to
   meet me.
As I walk down Bahnhofstrasse, church bells ring
   the air with their noon bouquets,
and everyone rushes about. I cross the street

to avoid the crowd around a street flautist,
sidestep a No. 9 tram that clangs a warning at me,
and then I am at the fountain, plunging my hands
into the water, cupping them for a drink.

Soon you will come and we will walk up the steps
   to the Lindenhof,
where we will share our lunch and look down on
   the city beneath us.
You will tell me about your day so far, and I you
   mine.
Then we will wander down to Daeniker's
   Bookshop
and I'll peruse the English books, but buy nothing,
and then we'll both return to our tasks,
until evening comes on
and the city lights shimmer on the dark gown of
   the lake,
and we walk home in the cold air filling now with
   snow.

# THE MAGICIAN

He pulls scarves out of his eyes
his eyes out of scarves

Too easy he thinks
the audience not impressed

So he puts a rabbit in a hat
a hat in a rabbit

Still too easy he thinks
the audience not impressed

So he reaches deep into the pocket
of his dead mother's womb

and out pops the world
dripping and wailing

Too easy he thinks
the audience not impressed

So he raises the dripping world
and spins it on his finger

The oceans bulge, the moon
wheels in its orbit

The stars scatter like ants
from a stomped mound

But the audience yawns
the audience turns away

So he stuffs the world
the moon stars ants

deep into his mouth
his mouth deep into

his body, his body
deeper into his mouth, deeper . . .

Then hears a faint rustling of leaves
which he mistakes for applause

# THE TOPSY-TURVY SUICIDE

With an eye out for architecture
I step from my window, lift the gray
sky like a hat to the rooftops, brown, green,
rust-red, and the church steeples, modern, old,
it doesn't matter, they spike the mountainous,
rain-veiled horizon, which I want to paint
with this pencil a shade too gray, a tint
too cold, so that from this new foundation
the right can wrong itself for the first
and last time, while topsy-turvy I tip my
slender self to my surrounds, bow out.

## COSMOLOGY

Your father drags you and your brother
Into a late afternoon field.
To each of you
He gives a stick
And makes you beat one another
Until you see stars.

## AUBADE (II)

The day begins when dream-worn sheets wake
the complexities of blood. The sun's imprint
on the blinds, or is it the moon intent
on lingering on some blanched lake
rippling with our desires? Are mistakes
of memory what the dark invents
for us to feed on? Counterfeit once spent
on phantasms forever circulates
the channel of our days, into which we
drift, pale leaves on a river of light,
ghosts of ghosts. And *this* is reality?
Or what's left—a hand on a child's head,
the laying of the evening meal—then night
like an old wife enters, turns back the bed.